It's My State! ★ ★ ★ ★ ★

COLORADO

The Centennial State

Linda Altman and Stephanie Fitzgerald

Cavendish Square

New York

Published in 2015 by Cavendish Square Publishing, LLC
243 5th Avenue, Suite 136, New York, NY 10016

Library of Congress Cataloging-in-Publication Data
Altman, Linda Jacobs, 1943-
 Colorado / Linda Altman, Stephanie Fitzgerald. — Third edition.
     pages cm. — (It's my state!)
 Includes index.
 ISBN 978-1-62712-482-9 (hardcover) ISBN 978-1-62712-485-0 (ebook)
 1. Colorado—Juvenile literature. I. Fitzgerald, Stephanie. II. Title.

 F776.3.A45 2014
 978.8—dc23

2014010505

Editorial Director: Dean Miller
Editor, Third Edition: Nicole Sothard
Art Director: Jeffrey Talbot
Series Designer, Third Edition: Jeffrey Talbot
Layout Design, Third Edition: Erica Clendening
Production Manager: Jennifer Ryder-Talbot

Printed in the United States of America

COLORADO
CONTENTS

A QUICK LOOK AT

State Flower: Rocky Mountain Columbine

This small and delicate columbine grows in the rugged Rocky Mountains. Edwin James discovered it in 1820, when he led the first successful climb of Pikes Peak. On April 4, 1899, the Rocky Mountain columbine became the official state flower.

State Bird: Lark Bunting

The perky little lark bunting is native to Colorado's eastern grasslands. It arrives each year in springtime and flies south in September. The males have a spectacular mating song of warbles and trills.

State Tree: Colorado Blue Spruce

The majestic blue spruce is named for its silvery blue color. A truly giant specimen can be found in Colorado's Gunnison National Forest. It is more than 126 feet (38 meters) high and measures 5 feet (1.5 m) around the trunk.

COLORADO

★ State Fossil: Stegosaurus

Colorado's state fossil is the plant-eating dinosaur stegosaurus. The Denver Museum of Nature and Science displays one of the most complete skeletons ever found. The bones of this plate-backed dinosaur were discovered in 1937 by a group of high school students and their teacher during a field trip.

★ State Insect: Colorado Hairstreak Butterfly

The hairstreak butterfly became Colorado's official insect on April 17, 1996. This tiny, brightly colored butterfly adds a flash of beauty to the Colorado mountainside.

★ State Animal: Rocky Mountain Bighorn Sheep

The Rocky Mountain bighorn sheep became Colorado's official state animal on May 1, 1961. The male bighorn stands about 3 feet (1 m) at the shoulder and may weigh as much as 300 pounds (136 kilograms). Its magnificent curving horns make it instantly identifiable.

Eagle Nest Rock near Fort Collins, in Northern Colorado.

The Centennial State

Colorado is a place of contrasts. The state is made up of 64 counties, which include rugged western landscapes, soaring mountain ranges, and flat grassland prairies. With an average elevation of 6,800 feet (2,100 kilometers) above sea level, Colorado is the highest state in the nation.

The state is commonly divided into four geographical regions: the Eastern Plains, the Front Range—or the Piedmont, as it is sometimes called—the Rocky Mountains, and the Colorado **Plateau**. Each of these regions has its own special features.

The Eastern Plains

The Eastern Plains of Colorado are part of the Great Plains region of the central United States. This vast grassland prairie is flat and dry. It is subject to howling winds and long periods of drought, or lack of water. The land is used for farming and raising livestock.

Rainfall averages 15 to 20 inches (38-51 centimeters) per year, but it comes in spurts. Weeks of dryness can be followed by days of rain and hail. Eastern Colorado farmers use both **irrigation** and dryland farming methods to make their land productive.

Like most farming areas, eastern Colorado is not heavily populated. It is a place of farms and small towns, with an average of about five people per square mile.

The sandstone shapes in the Garden of the Gods were formed by erosion.

Colorado Borders

North:	Wyoming Nebraska
South:	New Mexico Oklahoma
East:	Nebraska Kansas
West:	Utah

The Front Range

The Front Range stands between the Eastern Plains and the western mountains. It is about 50 miles (80 km) wide and 275 miles (445 km) long. Its elevation ranges from 4,921 to 14,110 feet (1,500 to 4,300 m) above sea level. The terrain is rugged, with many different landforms. There are cone-shaped "tepee buttes" and **mesas** with flat tops and steep sides. The mysterious and beautiful Garden of the Gods is located just west of Colorado Springs. Still farther west, on the edge of the Front Range of the Rocky Mountains, lies Pikes Peak.

The red sandstone formations in the Garden of the Gods were formed by **erosion**. Over time, wind and water carved the soft stone into fantastic shapes that look like ordinary objects. Famous landmarks include elephant rock (you can even see its trunk!), balanced rock, and sleeping giant. When two surveyors came upon the area in 1859, they were struck by its beauty. One of them mentioned that it was "a fit place for the gods to assemble." The man, Rufus Cable, named the spot Garden of the Gods.

Two formations at the entry to the garden frame a large purple mountain in the distance. That is Pikes Peak, standing like a guard at the edge of the Rocky Mountains. At 14,110 feet (4,300 m) above sea level, Pikes Peak is the thirty-first-highest peak in Colorado. It is the most visited mountain in North America. Two hundred years ago, **prospectors** in their wagon trains saw it and knew they had reached their goal.

Pikes Peak was named for Zebulon Pike. In 1806, he was the first American explorer to see it, but he never reached the top. He set out to climb the peak but was forced back by a blizzard. Edwin James made the first successful climb in recorded history in 1820.

Many pioneers never made it beyond Pikes Peak and into the Rockies. They settled in the Front Range instead, drawn by the cool climate, fresh mountain air, and beautiful surroundings.

Today, about 82 percent of Colorado's people live in this region. The state's largest cities—Denver, Colorado Springs, Aurora, and Lakewood—are there. Denver, the state capital, is the largest city in Colorado. It is nicknamed "the mile-high city" because its elevation is 5,280 feet (1,610 m)—exactly one mile above sea level.

Denver is one of the few cities that was not built on a road, railroad, lake, or body of water. It was founded in an area where gold was discovered.

COLORADO
COUNTY MAP

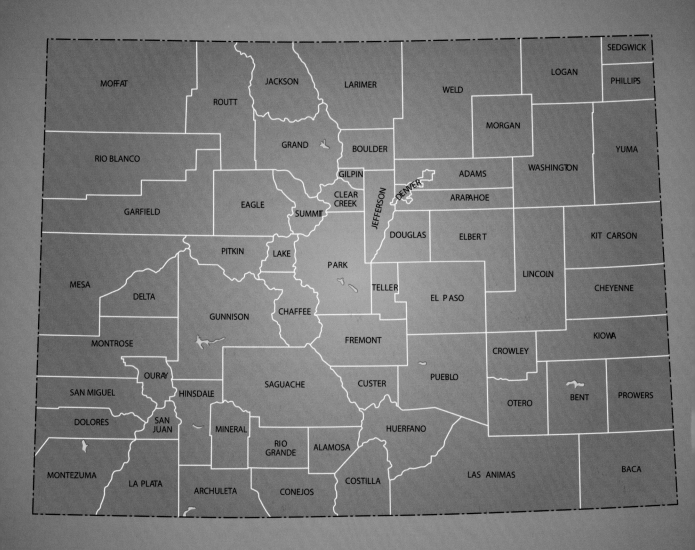

COLORADO
POPULATION BY COUNTY

County	Population	County	Population	County	Population
Adams County	441,603	Huerfano County	6,711	San Juan County	699
Alamosa County	15,445	Jackson County	1,394	San Miguel County	7,359
Arapahoe County	572,003	Jefferson County	534,543	Sedgwick County	2,379
Archuleta County	12,084	Kiowa County	1,398	Summit County	27,994
Baca County	3,788	Kit Carson County	8,270	Teller County	23,350
Bent County	6,499	Lake County	7,310	Washington County	4,814
Boulder County	294,567	La Plata County	51,334	Weld County	252,825
Broomfield County	55,889	Larimer County	299,630	Yuma County	10,043
Chaffee County	17,809	Las Animas County	15,507		
Cheyenne County	1,836	Lincoln County	5,467		
Clear Creek County	9,088	Logan County	22,709		
Conejos County	8,256	Mesa County	146,723		
Costilla County	3,524	Mineral County	712		
Crowley County	5,823	Moffat County	13,795		
Custer County	4,255	Montezuma County	25,535		
Delta County	30,952	Montrose County	41,276		
Denver County	600,158	Morgan County	28,159		
Dolores County	2,064	Otero County	18,831		
Douglas County	285,465	Ouray County	4,436		
Eagle County	52,197	Park County	16,206		
Elbert County	23,086	Phillips County	4,442		
El Paso County	622,263	Pitkin County	17,148		
Fremont County	46,824	Prowers County	12,551		
Garfield County	56,389	Pueblo County	159,063		
Gilpin County	5,441	Rio Blanco County	6,666		
Grand County	14,843	Rio Grande County	11,982		
Gunnison County	15,324	Routt County	23,509		
Hinsdale County	843	Saguache County	6,108		

Source: U.S. Bureau of the Census, 2010

Montezuma County

San Miguel County

There are more than 100 mountain ranges in the Rocky Mountains.

The Rocky Mountains

The Rocky Mountains are called the backbone of North America because the Continental Divide runs through them. Rivers east of the divide flow toward the Atlantic Ocean and the Gulf of Mexico. Rivers to the west of the divide flow toward the Pacific. The Rockies are not a single mountain range but a group of more than 100 individual ranges. They run a distance of approximately 3,000 miles (4,800 km). The Rockies stretch from northern Alberta, Canada, all the way down into New Mexico.

The Colorado Rockies are grouped into two large "belts" running north and south through the center of the state. The belts are separated by a series of high mountain valleys. At least 1,000 peaks in the Colorado Rockies are more than 10,000 feet

(3,000 m) above sea level. Fifty-four are over 14,000 feet (4,300 m) high. Almost no one lives in the upper reaches of those 54 mountains. Even the bighorn sheep leave in winter, seeking lower—and warmer—territory.

The Rockies as a whole are sparsely populated, averaging only two people per square mile (2.59 sq km). The population is concentrated in the high mountain valleys, where level ground makes farming and ranching possible. There are no major cities in the Colorado Rockies, but there are a number of thriving small towns.

Two of Colorado's best-known mountain towns are Aspen and Leadville. Both began as silver mining towns and were almost destroyed when the mining boom ended. However, both survived, and they have grown into very popular resort towns.

The Colorado Plateau

The Colorado Plateau is a truly western landscape. It is a place of mountains and mesas, valleys and canyons. Along the western slope of the Rockies are woodlands of juniper and piñon pine. Farther west, trees give way to semidesert shrub lands.

Like the high mountains and the Eastern Plains, western Colorado is thinly populated. Its largest city is Grand Junction, with more than 58,000 people. Orchards and vineyards dominate the landscape around Grand Junction. With irrigation, western Colorado provides ideal conditions for wine grapes. Peaches, cherries, and nectarines are also grown there.

The Colorado Plateau, in the western part of the state, is not heavily populated.

Denver Botanic Gardens

Denver Zoo

Garden of the Gods

1. Denver Botanic Gardens at York Street

The Denver Botanic Gardens at York Street feature more than 700 species of plants from Colorado and western North America. There are also programs that focus on protecting and preserving the wildlife that these beautiful gardens celebrate.

2. Denver Museum of Nature and Science

This natural history and science museum features programs, exhibits, and activities that teach visitors about the natural history of Colorado, Earth, and outer space. Some of the museum's exhibits focus on dinosaurs, Egyptian history, and gems and minerals. There is also a planetarium.

3. Denver Zoo

In 1918, the Denver Zoo became the first zoo in America to feature natural habitats for its animals rather than cages. Today, visitors can see a wide range of animals, such as tigers, grizzly bears, komodo dragons, and fish.

4. Dinosaur National Monument

The Dinosaur Quarry Exhibit Hall contains 1,500 fossils and the Carnegie Fossil Quarry produced the remains of eleven different dinosaur species such as allosaurus, diplodocus, and stegosaurus. You can view petroglyphs and pictographs or go river rafting.

5. Garden of the Gods

This park located near Colorado Springs features tall red, pink, and white rock formations that are millions of years old. Visitors can tour the park, learn about its history at the visitor center, hike, bike, and go horseback riding as well.

COLORADO

6. Glenwood Hot Springs

The natural hot springs in Glenwood Springs, the town where gunfighter Doc Holiday is buried, are thought to be therapeutic. There are 3.5 million gallons (11.3 milliliters) of mineral water that pass through the pool each day. There are water slides and a kiddy pool among other amenities.

7. Mesa Verde National Park

Located in Montezuma County, Mesa Verde National Park gives visitors a look at how the Ancient Pueblo people lived in the area from 600 to 1300 CE. The park has more than 5,000 archeological sites, including around 600 cliff dwellings.

8. Pikes Peak

Pikes Peak is a mountain west of Colorado Springs. The 19-mile (31-km) Pikes Peak Highway leads visitors to an elevation of 14,115 feet (4,302 m). Once at the top, you can see breathtaking views of the Rocky Mountains and surrounding Colorado scenery.

9. Red Rocks Amphitheatre

Opened in 1941, Red Rocks Amphitheatre, near Morrison, features hiking, tours, shopping, and dining. However, it is most famous for its summer concerts held at the Amphitheatre. The surrounding red rocks make the area acoustically perfect.

10. Rocky Mountain National Park

This 415 square mile (1,075 sq km) park is one of the most spectacular parks in the United States. Visitors can view mountain peaks, lakes, forests, and wildlife. Popular sites include Longs Peak, Trail Ridge Road, and Bear Lake.

Mesa Verde National Park

Pikes Peak

Red Rocks Ampitheatre

Grand Lake is the largest natural lake in Colorado.

Tepee Buttes

A tepee butte is a hill or knoll that is shaped like a tepee. It has a small summit area (or top) and very steep sides.

Three famous sites in western Colorado are Mesa Verde National Park, Four Corners National Monument, and Dinosaur National Monument. At Mesa Verde—Spanish for "green table"—ancient cliff dwellings seem to grow out of the rock. The structures were created by a people known today as the Ancestral Pueblo people. The park has more than 4,000 archaeological sites containing the remains of ancient human habitation. The remains date back to 600 CE.

The Four Corners National Monument is the only place in the country where a person can be in four different states at the same time. The monument is located on the Navajo Reservation at the point where Arizona, Colorado, New Mexico, and Utah meet. This point is called a quadripoint.

Dinosaur National Monument is one of the largest dinosaur fossil sites in the world. Earl Douglass, a paleontologist (a scientist who studies prehistoric life), found the quarry in 1909. Over the years, the quarry has yielded thousands of bones, including many nearly complete skeletons. The site also contains rock art—petroglyphs and pictographs—made by the Fremont people who lived in the area 800 to 1,200 years ago.

Rivers and Lakes

The biggest lakes in Colorado are reservoirs, which were created by damming the flow of mountain streams. Blue Mesa Reservoir is the largest of these artificial lakes, covering about 29 square miles (75 square km). There are dozens of natural lakes in the mountains. The largest of them, Grand Lake, covers about one square mile (2.6 sq km). The Ute tribe named it Spirit Lake because they believed the souls of those who had died lived in the lake's cold waters.

Colorado is the birthplace of four major rivers. The Colorado River begins west of the Continental Divide. It flows southwest for 1,470 miles (2,370 km) to the Sea of Cortez. The Rio Grande is located east of the Divide, as are the South Platte River, which flows into the Missouri, and the Arkansas River, which flows into the Mississippi.

Climate

On Colorado's Eastern Plains, summers are hot, winters are cold, and rainfall is scarce. In central and western Colorado, **altitude** determines the type of weather and average temperature. For example, the winter temperature in the high mountain city of Leadville averages 24 degrees Fahrenheit (-4 degrees Celsius). The plains town of Colorado Springs averages about 31 °F (-0.6 °C). In July, differences are even more pronounced, with Leadville averaging 53 °F (12 °C) and Colorado Springs 68 °F (20 °C).

Annual snowfall also shows how climate is related to elevation in Colorado. Leadville can receive more than 200 inches (508 cm) of snow a year, while Colorado Springs gets around 42 inches (107 cm). A Rocky Mountain blizzard is something to behold. For example, in 1990, a single storm dropped 50 inches (127 cm) of snow at Echo Lake in north-central Colorado. Wind-driven snow brought traffic to a stop on the highway between Boulder and Denver.

Burrowing owls are a threatened species in Colorado.

One of Colorado's strangest weather patterns is the chinook wind. A chinook wind is warm and dry, swooping down from the mountains at near-hurricane speeds. One can raise the temperature 40 or 50 degrees Fahrenheit (22.2 to 27.8 degrees Celsius) in an hour's time.

Wildlife

From the plains to the plateau, Colorado's wildlife is varied and interesting. The Eastern Plains have small mammals such as rabbits, prairie dogs, skunks, and ground squirrels, along with the coyotes that feed on them.

Wherever there are prairie dogs, there will be burrowing owls. These small brown owls live in abandoned prairie dog burrows. Burrowing owls are on Colorado's list of threatened species. Their habitat is shrinking, partly because development is destroying prairie dog towns. Colorado's Partners in Flight program has created a **conservation** plan. It includes protecting burrows and reducing the use of insecticides, especially during the owls' breeding season.

Colorado's mountains are home to elk, moose, and bighorn sheep. Foxes, badgers, and beavers also thrive in the region. Bears may also be found, but only a few of these creatures live year-round at the highest altitudes. Like the bighorn sheep, some of these bears move to lower altitudes for winter.

The animals of western Colorado have at least one trait in common. All can survive in a land of little rainfall. Porcupines, weasels, hares, and mule deer live where the juniper and piñon pine give way to sand and sagebrush. Predators that hunt these animals include coyotes, bobcats, and mountain lions. Golden eagles may also be found in this area.

Mountain lions are rare, but they can be found in Colorado.

10 KEY PLANTS AND ANIMALS

Aspen

Bald Eagle

Juniper

1. Aspen

The aspen is Colorado's only widespread, native **deciduous** tree. It is most commonly found in the western two-thirds of the state. The tree has a grayish-white trunk and green leaves that turn a beautiful yellow-gold color in mid-September.

2. Bald Eagle

Two decades ago, bald eagles were extremely rare in the lower 48 states. Thanks to conservation efforts in Colorado, however, the state had more than a hundred breeding pairs in 2008, and sightings have become increasingly common. These majestic birds live high up in the trees, near reservoirs or other large waterways. They feed on fish and small mammals.

3. State Tree: Colorado Blue Spruce

The Colorado blue spruce can grow to be around 60 to 80 feet (18-24 m) tall. Colorado school children voted to name the blue spruce the state tree on Arbor Day in 1892, but it did not become official until 1939.

4. Elk

The elk is related to the deer, but is much larger. A male can grow to be 9 feet (2.7 m) tall. This includes its antlers, which can rise 4 feet (1.2 m) above the elk's head. Elk live in higher elevations during the summer and lower elevations during the winter.

5. Juniper

Different types of juniper grow across the state. These evergreen shrubs produce red berries that provide food for Colorado's wildlife. Humans, however, should never eat these berries. They can be poisonous.

COLORADO

6. State Bird: Lark Bunting

Male lark buntings are black with large white patches on their wings. Females are sandy colored with a white belly and black streaks. They are often seen in large groups, and they eat seeds and insects.

7. Lynx

This large cat has grayish-brown fur and tufts of hair at the tops of its ears. By 1973, it seemed as if the lynx had disappeared from Colorado. A restoration program was started in 1999. By 2005, more than 200 lynxes had been released into the wild, and a number of litters had been born.

8. Moose

Colorado's moose live in some of the state's forests and are most often found in North Park. An adult moose can weigh more than 1,000 pounds (455 kg). Moose have long legs that are good for walking through deep snow. They eat mainly plant material such as leaves, berries, and grasses.

9. State Animal: Rocky Mountain Bighorn Sheep

Bighorn sheep, also known as rams, are known for their curved horns. Males often use their horns to fight each other over mating rights. Both bighorn sheep stand on their back legs, and they hurl at each other at around 20 miles (32 km) an hour.

10. State Flower: Rocky Mountain Columbine

The Rocky Mountain columbine has blue-violet petals, a white cup, and yellow center. Blue represents the sky, white represents snow, and gold symbolizes Colorado's mining history. The flower has a strong scent, which attracts hummingbirds, bees, and butterflies.

Lynx

Moose

Rocky Mountain Bighorn Sheep

The Ancestral Pueblo people built homes into the cliffs of Colorado.

From the Beginning

Colorado's first people, known as Paleo-Indians, arrived about 13,000 years ago. They hunted mastodons, mammoths, and other gigantic creatures. When big game became scarce, the Paleo-Indians turned to hunting smaller game. They also began gathering plant matter to supplement their diets.

The **descendants** of these early people were also hunter-gatherers. The descendants used to be called Anasazi, which is a Navajo word meaning "enemies of our **ancestors**." Today, the preferred term is Ancestral Pueblo people. From 500 BCE to about 800 CE, these ancient peoples were known as Basket Makers, because they made beautiful baskets that had many uses. The next phase of the people's history, 800 CE until about 1300 CE, was known as the Puebloan era. During this time, the Ancestral Pueblo people built magnificent homes into the cliff faces of southwestern Colorado and farmed the land above. Some of these homes are still standing today. Other native peoples, including the Ute, Comanche, Cheyenne, Arapaho, and Kiowa, also made their homes in what is now Colorado. They lived undisturbed by outsiders until the first Spanish explorers arrived in the early sixteenth century.

Beautifully preserved Native American structures and artifacts can be seen in Mesa Verde National Park.

These explorers were followed in time by settlers who came for the land, and fortune seekers who came for the silver and gold. All played a part in the often stormy history of the Centennial State.

The Earliest Settlers

The Ancestral Pueblo people have long been a mystery to archaeologists. Exactly who were they? How did they learn to build magnificent, multistory "apartment houses"? Why did they suddenly abandon it all and seemingly disappear? Nobody knows all the answers to these questions. What scientists and historians do know is that the Ancestral Pueblo people were hunters and gatherers. They also made pottery and developed farming techniques. The Ancestral Pueblo people built their homes using sandstone rocks held together with adobe (sun-dried clay and straw). Many of these homes are extraordinary cliff dwellings. The remains of these magnificent structures can still be seen in Mesa Verde National Park.

No one knows for certain why the Ancestral Pueblo people seem to have disappeared. Some **scholars** blame a long drought that destroyed the crops. Many think that the Ancestral Pueblo people migrated out of the area to join other native cultures.

The Pueblo, a Native American group found in the Southwest, are the descendants of the Ancestral Pueblo people.

Long after the Ancestral Pueblo people were gone, other Native American peoples continued to settle in what is now Colorado. These included the Cheyenne, Kiowa, Arapaho, Comanche, and Ute. Most of these natives were hunters and gatherers. They often followed the buffalo herds on the Eastern Plains, bringing along their homes and families.

The Ute favored higher altitudes. Some of them lived 10,000 feet (3,050 m) above sea level. For food they gathered wild plants and fished in the rivers and streams. They also hunted elk and deer, using the meat for food and using the hides for their homes and clothing. Later, the Ute traded the hides and other goods for horses and other necessities. The Ute were skilled riders and used horses for hunting. But life for all the Native American groups in the region began to change as European explorers and settlers arrived in greater numbers.

The Ute often moved their camps as they hunted large prey.

The Native People

The Ute are the oldest Native tribe originally from Colorado. There was a group of Ancient Pueblo People who built the cliff dwellings in the southwest corner of the state, but they left the area around 1300 CE. Migration added the Apache, Arapaho, Comanche, Cheyenne, Shoshone, and Pueblo tribes to the state by the time the Spanish arrived in the 1500s.

The Pueblo tribes, such as the Navajo, lived in villages in homes made of mud, and grew corn, beans, peppers, and other vegetables. The other tribes lived on the Great Plains and were more nomadic. Their homes were either wickiups or tepees. Wickiups were wood framed and covered with brush, and could be made in a few hours. The tepees were conical, with wood poles meeting at the top and covered with buffalo skins. The women built the homes, and were responsible for dragging the frames when the tribe moved. The men were primarily hunters, seeking buffalo, deer, antelope, and small game. The Plains tribes originally used dogs to pull their belongings when they moved, but when the Spanish brought horses to North America they became skilled riders.

The arrival of settlers from the East brought conflict for the Native people in Colorado and elsewhere in the West. With tensions rising, a band of Colonel John Chivington's Colorado volunteers attacked a settlement of Arapaho families on November 29, 1864, in what is known as the Sand Creek Massacre. To subdue the tribes, the U.S. army set up a system to allow hunters to slaughter the buffalo, the main source of food for the Great Plains tribes, and to sell the hides. The buffalo population fell from at least thirty million in the 1860s to less than 400 by 1893. The Native Americans were unable to feed themselves and were confined to reservations, some in Colorado but many in Oklahoma.

Today the Native population of Colorado is estimated at close to 80,500. There are two federally recognized tribes in Colorado today, the Southern Ute Tribe and the Ute Mountain Ute Tribe.

Spotlight on the Arapaho

The Arapaho is a tribe that lived in the plains region of Colorado. After gold was discovered near Denver in 1858, confrontations between the tribe and white settlers intensified. A treaty in 1861 attempted to remove the southern branch of the tribe, but it was never ratified, or approved.

This illustration shows an Arapaho village of tepees.

Food: The Arapaho diet consisted of mostly meat, such as buffalo, deer, and elk that they hunted. The tribe also gathered food, such as berries, vegetables, and roots. Hunting not only provided food, but it provided materials for shelter, clothing, and trading.

Clothing: Arapaho women wore leggings and dresses. They used paint, porcupine quills, elk teeth, and beads for decoration. Arapaho men wore breechcloths, or loincloths, shirts (sometimes), leggings, and moccasins.

Powwows: Powwows, which began in the mid-1800s, were social gatherings that featured competitive dancing and honoring ceremonies. Powwows still happen around the country today.

Sun Dance: The Sun Dance is a ceremony during which the Arapaho pray to their higher powers. It generally takes place during the summer, and it lasts around seven days, of which the last four days involve the dancing. It was, and still is, one of the tribe's most sacred ceremonies.

This photo shows two men setting a bear trap. Animal pelts were sold to make clothing and other goods.

European Exploration

In 1682, a French explorer named René-Robert Cavelier, sieur de La Salle, claimed a huge area of land in central North America for France. La Salle himself never visited the region that is now Colorado; he simply claimed everything between the Mississippi River and the Rocky Mountains. The territory extended northward to the present-day Canadian border and south to the Gulf of Mexico. La Salle named this vast region "Louisiana" in honor of King Louis XIV of France.

The Spanish were the first Europeans to actually explore Colorado. In 1706, Juan de Ulibarri led an expedition as far as present-day Pueblo. He promptly claimed the "new" territory for Spain.

American Claims on Colorado

In 1803, the United States bought the whole Louisiana Territory from France for $15 million. With one purchase—which became known as the Louisiana Purchase—President Thomas Jefferson doubled the size of the country. The next step was to explore this new addition.

That job fell, in part, to a 26-year-old army lieutenant named Zebulon Pike. In 1806, Pike set out to explore the southwestern borders of the Louisiana Purchase. It was on this trip that he discovered the peak that bears his name. Pike also had a secret mission. Spain had conquered and settled all of Mexico and most of the present-day American Southwest, including part of Colorado. The U.S. government asked Pike to check the strength of Spanish settlements in the region. Pike investigated the situation, traveling south from Colorado to the area that now includes New Mexico. He and his men were arrested by Spanish authorities and taken to Santa Fe, New Mexico, but they were later released by the Spanish.

Because of the Pike incident, the United States and Spain held talks about the boundaries of the Louisiana Purchase. In 1819, a treaty between the two nations gave northern and eastern Colorado to the United States, and southern and western Colorado to Spain.

In 1821, Mexico won its independence from Spain. It acquired all the Spanish territory in what is now the United States, including parts of Colorado. The new Mexican government did not have the resources to develop this large area, so it welcomed Americans into the Rocky Mountain wilderness.

"The Gregory Lode"

In 1859, John Gregory discovered gold in a gulch near Central City. Within two weeks, the gold rush began. Within two months, the population grew to 10,000. It came to be known as "The Richest Square Mile on Earth."

The Mountain Men

A group of sturdy adventurers who became known as mountain men gladly accepted the invitation. They were strong, hearty men who lived by trapping beaver and other fur-bearing animals. The pelts were sold to make clothing and other goods.

The mountain men came from all over the United States and Canada. Some were interested in exploring, and some just hoped to make a profit from this new land. Many of them had little or no education, but they were wise in the ways of nature. They often served as guides, trackers, and scouts.

Making a Model Stegosaurus

Colorado's state fossil is the stegosaurus. It lived in the western part of the United States around 150 million years ago. The plant-eating stegosaurus was about the size of a bus, but the plates on its back and tail made it look even bigger. Follow these steps to make a stegosaurus of your own!

What You Need

Baking clay in red, yellow, orange, and brown
Toothpick
Metal baking sheet

What To Do

- Preheat your oven to 275°F (130°C).
- Knead the clay until soft and smooth.
- For best results, clean your hands in between colors.
- Using yellow clay, make four thick clubs for the legs. Flatten one end to make the feet.
- Also using the yellow clay, make one thick piece for the body. Pull one end into a point for the tail. Round the other end and make it thinner for the head. Draw a mouth with the toothpick.
- Using red clay, make eight small triangles for the back spikes, four teardrops for the tail spikes, and one flattened ball for the tongue.
- Using orange clay, make two flattened balls for the eyes and 10-20 balls for the spikes' spots.
- Using brown clay, make two tiny circles for the pupils of the eyes.
- Press the legs to the sides of the body. Press the spikes onto the back and the end of the tail.
- Add the tongue, eyes, and pupils to the head.
- Add the spots to the spikes.
- Have an adult help you with the next step. Bake the stegosaurus on the baking sheet for 15 minutes per 0.25-inch (6 millimeter) thickness.
- Allow to cool when finished.

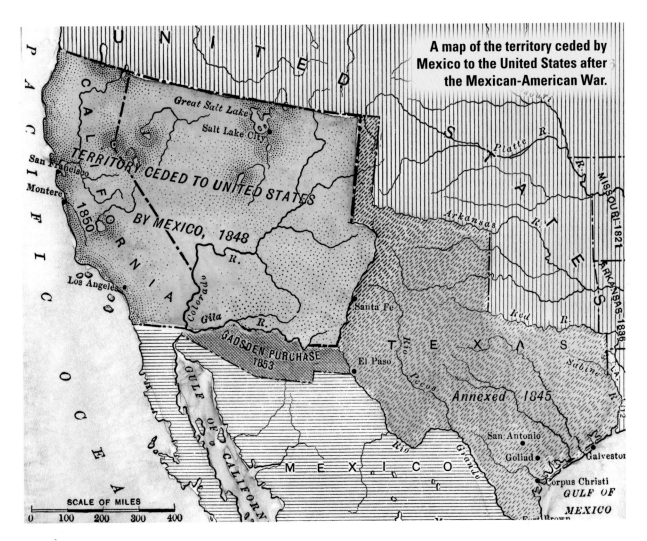

A map of the territory ceded by Mexico to the United States after the Mexican-American War.

The mountain men knew that the Native Americans still controlled the land in Colorado, and for the most part, they respected the indigenous peoples' rights. White settlement was limited to a few trading posts or forts. Both mountain men and Native Americans traded at these outposts. One of the best-known posts was Bent's Fort in southeastern Colorado, near the present-day town of La Junta. The legendary tracker Kit Carson once worked there. His title was chief hunter, and his job was to keep the fort well supplied with meat.

In the 1840s, the world of the mountain men began to change. Because of overtrapping, beaver populations had shrunk. Changes in fashion also made beaver fur less popular. Without as many beaver and with a smaller demand for the pelts, making a living as a trapper became very hard. This issue, combined with disaster and disease, caused the abandonment of Bent's Fort in 1849.

After the United States defeated Mexico in the Mexican-American War, which lasted from 1846 to 1848, Mexico gave up almost all of its territory in the American Southwest to

The trip west was a dangerous one. Many pioneers did not make it to Pikes Peak.

the United States for $15 million. Besides part of Colorado, the territory included all of present-day California, Nevada, and Utah, and parts of Arizona, New Mexico, and Wyoming. In 1853, an additional U.S. purchase of almost 30,000 square miles (77,700 sq km) of land in what is now southern Arizona and New Mexico would give the continental United States (excluding Alaska) its present borders.

"Pikes Peak or Bust!"

In January 1848, gold was discovered in California, starting one of the largest human migrations in history. During the "gold rush," about 500,000 people hoping to strike it rich headed for California. Many of these people passed through Colorado on their quest for gold. In 1858, a party led by miner William Green Russell found gold at Dry Creek, just south of the present-day site of Denver. This brought more prospectors to the area and was followed by three larger finds in Colorado in 1859. Thousands of people tacked "Pikes Peak or Bust" signs on their wagons and headed west to make their fortunes. Towns sprang up almost overnight. Montana City, Denver City, and Auraria became the core of modern Denver.

Through the 1860s, miners struck gold in different parts of Colorado. In 1860, gold was found in Leadville, one of Colorado's famous mining towns. In 1875, prospectors found a large deposit of lead carbonite ore there. The ore contained large quantities of silver. It was only the first of many silver discoveries in the area. By 1878, the city of Leadville had become one of the most important mining camps in the nation. It produced a crop of overnight millionaires.

The most famous of these mining millionaires was Horace Tabor, the Silver King. Tabor went from storekeeper to millionaire in 1877 when he "grubstaked" two prospectors, or gave them tools and supplies in exchange for a share of anything they found at the Little Pittsburgh Mine. What they found was silver—lots of it. Tabor grubstaked several other expeditions, and his fortune grew. In late 1879, he bought the Matchless Mine for $117,000. People thought he was crazy because the Matchless had plunged its previous owners into debt and returned nothing. But Tabor had a hunch, and he was right. By the spring of 1880, the Matchless was producing a $2,000 profit each day. Tabor became the richest of all the silver millionaires.

The good times in Leadville ended in 1893, when a severe economic depression hit the country. The government stopped buying silver to make coins. The price of silver dropped. Tabor and many other miners lost nearly everything.

This sketch shows the booming city of Leadville in the early 1880s.

10 KEY CITIES

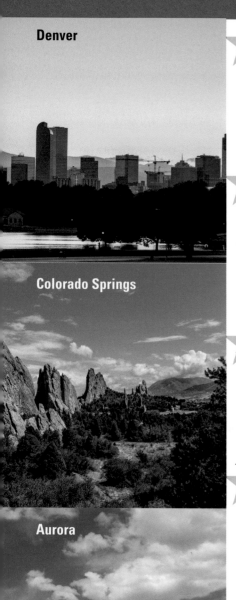

Denver

Colorado Springs

Aurora

1. Denver: population 600,158

Denver, the state capital, is the 23rd most populous city in America. It began as a mining town, but quickly grew in size. Today, it is a bustling city with many museums, music venues, and a lot of outdoor activities.

2. Colorado Springs: population 416,427

Located south of Denver, Colorado Springs is Colorado's largest city by area at 194.7 square miles (504 sq km). The city was named the number one best big city by *Money* magazine in 2006, and placed number one in *Outside* magazine's list of America's best cities in 2009.

3. Aurora: population 325,078

Aurora, located just outside Denver, has more than 100 parks, seven golf courses, 6,000 acres (2,428 hectares) of open space, and 50 miles (80 km) of hiking trails. There are also 26 historical sites and landmarks.

4. Fort Collins: population 143,986

Fort Collins, in Northern Colorado, was named America's best place to live in 2006 by *Money* magazine and number six in 2010. Fort Collins is also one of the towns that inspired the design of Main Street, U.S.A., one of the areas inside Disneyland and DisneyWorld.

5. Lakewood: population 142,980

Lakewood, southwest of Denver, has some of the best views of the Rocky Mountains. Known more as a suburb, Lakewood is slowly emerging as its own city with its own identity. A new downtown area, Belmar, attracts people to its shopping, dining, and music.

COLORADO

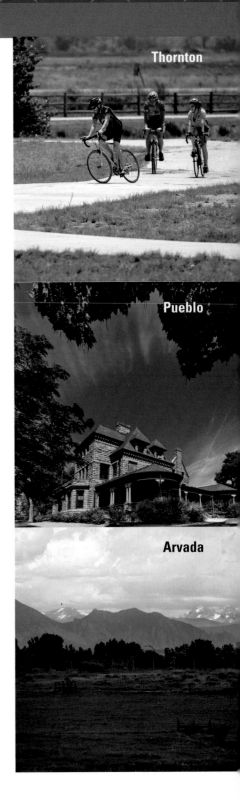

Thornton

Pueblo

Arvada

6. **Thornton: population 118,772**

Located north of Denver, Thornton is also known as a suburb of the major city. Thornton has plenty to do, though. With around 80 parks and 80 miles (130 km) of trails, residents and visitors enjoy the outdoors at home and the nearby Rocky Mountains.

7. **Pueblo: population 106,595**

Pueblo is nicknamed "Steel City" because it is one of the largest-producing steel cities in America. Pueblo is home to the Colorado State Fair, and it has a large Hispanic, Italian, and Slovenian population.

8. **Arvada: population 106,433**

Established in 1870, the city of Arvada has tree-lined streets, parks, trails, theater, art, and diverse businesses. Its downtown neighborhood is on the National Register of Historic Places.

9. **Westminster: population 106,114**

When gold was discovered nearby, settlers made their homes in the area during the 1850s. The town, once called Harris, was renamed Westminster after Westminster University, in 1911. Today, the area is known for its recreational activities, such as hiking and golf.

10. **Centennial: population 100,377**

This city located outside of Denver was named Centennial in honor of Colorado's admission to the Union in 1876. It was the centennial year, or 100 years after, the signing of the Declaration of Independence. Today, it is a quiet suburb and considered one of the safest cities in the state.

Silver miners rest near Silver Cliff, Colorado.

Colorado Territory

The mining boom was just under way when Colorado became a U.S. territory. The status became official on February 28, 1861. The new territory immediately created a **legislature**, or lawmaking body, called the Territorial Assembly. At its first meeting, the assembly created 17 counties, made plans for the University of Colorado, and chose Colorado City as the territorial capitol.

The influx of settlers became of increasing concern to Native Americans in the area. In 1851, ten years before Colorado became a territory, the United States signed the Great Horse Creek Treaty with the Cheyenne. The treaty stated that prospectors and settlers would not be allowed to **encroach** upon the

Cheyenne's traditional hunting grounds. By 1861, however, the newcomers were building houses, establishing towns, and stringing telegraph wires across the mountains and the prairies—right in the middle of the Cheyenne's land. Soldiers shot a Cheyenne chief in 1864, and the Native Americans responded with violence. Then, Colorado soldiers attacked and destroyed a village in Sand Creek. They brutally murdered hundreds of Cheyenne and Arapaho people, many fleeing for their lives. The Sand Creek Massacre, as it was later called, would lead to changes in federal Native American policies.

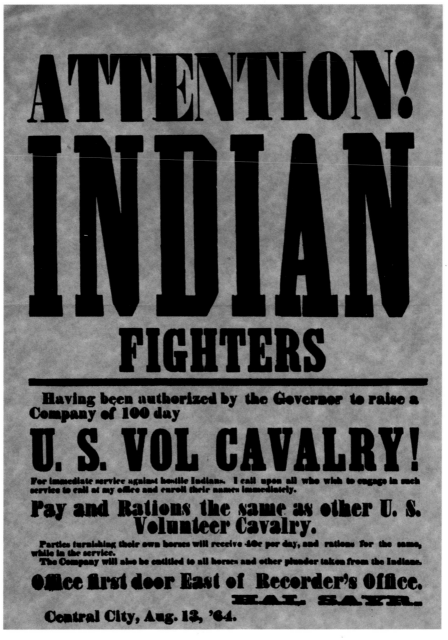

This poster from 1864 asked for volunteers to fight against Native Americans.

Settlers needed the presence of soldiers in Colorado even a year after the Great Horse Creek Treaty was signed. The relationship between settlers and Native Americans was tense for many years.

Fighting between settlers and Native Americans continued. The government forced many Cheyenne, Sioux, Arapaho, and Ute to move off their lands and onto reservations. Nathan C. Meeker, the federal agent in charge of the Ute reservation, tried to force the Ute to become farmers. In 1879, they rebelled, killing Meeker and others. The Meeker Massacre was the last big clash between Colorado's indigenous people and settlers. Army forces overpowered the Native Americans, who returned to the reservations.

Into a New Century

On August 1, 1876, Colorado became the thirty-eighth state to join the United States. The Leadville silver boom was already under way. Hopes ran high as Coloradans settled down to the business of building a state. More schools and universities were opened. Miles of new railroad tracks were laid down. Farmers developed dryland farming techniques on the plains. Dryland farming includes, among other things, planting drought-resistant crops, as well as increasing the water absorption and reducing the moisture loss from soil. By the turn of the twentieth century, Colorado had a population of 539,700 people. Mining and agriculture were important to the economy.

Colorado's mining industry survived the silver collapse of 1893, largely because of gold. A few gold strikes kept the industry going. Some mines also made money from coal and other minerals.

As Colorado's population grew, farmers found new ways to produce crops.

The coal mining town of Hastings suffered a devastating coal mine fire in 1917.

Farmers on the Eastern Plains used a combination of dryland farming methods and irrigation to develop the land. They produced good crops of sugar beets, as well as wheat and other grains.

When World War I (1914–1918) began, Great Britain and its allies in Europe needed raw materials. They bought food products from Colorado farms and metals such as tungsten and molybdenum from Colorado mines. When the

United States entered the war in 1917, Colorado farmers and miners increased production even more.

During the 1920s, Colorado built paved highways for automobile traffic and expanded its oil industry. By 1930, the state's population topped one million for the first time in history.

Also by 1930, the American stock market had collapsed and so had the economy of the nation. This began what came to be known as the Great Depression. In Colorado as elsewhere, many people lost their jobs and some lost their homes. The economy did not recover until the United States entered World War II in December 1941. The U.S. government decided that Colorado would be a safe location for military installations and other federal facilities. Soon, a number of government offices, defense plants, and military bases were located in the state. Many of them stayed after the war ended, and so did the people who staffed them. President Dwight D. Eisenhower established the U.S. Air Force Academy in 1954. Four years later, the Colorado Springs facility was ready to admit students.

Three girls stand in the snow in Denver. During the Depression, some people lost their homes and had to live in what were known as tent cities.

By 1960, Colorado's population had grown to more than 1.7 million. Three counties in the Front Range—Denver, Adams, and Jefferson—grew especially rapidly. The state's Eastern Plains lost people as quickly as the Front Range gained them. During the 1970s and 1980s, the suburbs around Denver became more heavily populated.

Throughout the 1980s and 1990s—and into the twenty-first century—the old standbys of mining and agriculture became less important to Colorado's economy. Old mining towns such as Aspen and Telluride found new life as expensive ski resorts. Technological industries flourished, and tourism became an important source of income for the state.

The U.S. Air Force Academy, located in Colorado Springs, was established in 1954.

10 KEY DATES IN STATE HISTORY

1. **800 CE to 1300 CE**
The culture of the Ancestral Pueblo people flourishes.

2. **April 9, 1682**
René-Robert Cavelier, sieur de La Salle claims a vast territory, which includes Colorado, for France.

3. **April 30, 1803**
The United States buys land, including part of Colorado, from France in the Louisiana Purchase. The U.S. pays more than $11 million.

4. **February 2, 1848**
In the Treaty of Guadalupe Hidalgo, Mexico cedes to the United States the remainder of Colorado that was not bought during the Louisiana Purchase. The United States pays Mexico $15 million.

5. **February 28, 1861**
The U.S. Territory of Colorado is officially established after the gold rush that began in Pikes Peak around 1858. During this time, many southern states are seceding from the Union, which leads to the Civil War.

6. **August 1, 1876**
After many years of attempts to become a state, Colorado becomes the thirty-eighth U.S. state.

7. **November 7, 1893**
Colorado becomes the second state, after Wyoming, to grant women the right to vote. Men passed the referendum overwhelmingly.

8. **January 25, 1998**
Quarterback John Elway leads the Denver Broncos to the first of two straight Super Bowl wins. Elway wins Most Valuable Player in the second game in 1999.

9. **August 25-28, 2008**
The Democratic National Convention is held in Denver. Barack Obama, the first African-American president of the United States, is officially nominated there.

10. **June 11, 2013**
The Black Forest Fire starts near Colorado Springs. It lasts for nine days and burns between 14,000 and 16,000 acres (5,666-6,475 ha) of land. More than 500 structures are destroyed. It is one of the worst forest fires in Colorado history.

Skiing is one of the most popular activities enjoyed by both residents and tourists in Colorado.

The People

In a state historically known for prospectors, trappers, and hardy pioneers, more than 80 percent of Coloradans live in cities. Many families still live in rural communities or on farms, but the cities and suburbs draw the most residents.

City living has not destroyed Coloradans' love for their "purple mountain majesties," however. Outdoor activities such as skiing, mountain biking, and river rafting are popular. As for taking care of their beautiful state, thousands of Coloradans are involved in environmental protection projects.

The Faces of Colorado

Since its days as a U.S. territory, Colorado has been home to a population that is largely Caucasian, or white. People of Hispanic descent have always made up the largest ethnic minority. They outnumber all other minority groups combined. The same ratio, or proportion, holds true today. Caucasians make up almost 82 percent of the population. Some are direct descendants of European and American explorers and settlers who came to the region hundreds of years ago. Others are from families that have lived in Colorado for the last few decades. Colorado residents may also come from different parts of the country. A portion of the Caucasian population in the state is of European descent. They

Native Americans make up about one percent of Colorado's population. This Ute woman works in a pottery factory.

may be from, or have family from, Great Britain, Scotland, Ireland, France, Germany, or Italy.

Native Americans

The people with the longest history in Colorado are today one of its smallest minority groups. Native Americans account for only about one percent of the population. More than 56,000 Native people live in the state, which is also home to two Ute reservations. The Southern Ute Reservation is located in south-central Colorado. The Ute Mountain Reservation is farther west and spreads into the neighboring states of Utah and New Mexico.

It can be a struggle for Native peoples to live in the modern world while still trying to hold on to their ancient traditions. Organizations such as the

Southern Ute Cultural Center can help. Through its museum, the group aims to be "the principal conservator and interpreter of our Tribe's history, our stories, our culture, and its artifacts." The Ute Mountain Tribal Park encompasses lands that contain native rock art and ancient dwellings. The Southern Utes also host a Bear Dance each spring, as well as a Sun Dance ceremony in the summer. The Bear Dance and the Sun Dance are both important ceremonies that have been practiced among the Utes for hundreds of years.

Still, in the hustle and bustle of modern life, the old ways can get lost. The Ute language has nearly disappeared. Only a handful of adults speak it, and the children are not learning it.

Teacher Stacey Oberly decided to do something about that. In 1999, she began teaching Ute to her kindergartners and first graders at a school on the Southern Ute Reservation. To make the learning fun, she held up flash cards of familiar objects, colors, and animals. The children would shout out the appropriate Ute word. Oberly knew that flash cards could not save the ancient language of her people. Still, for these five- and six-year-old students, it was a good start. "Maybe they'll remember a few words and take some pride in their culture," Oberly said.

A Ute father and daughter share a smile. Only a few of Colorado's people speak the Ute language.

10 KEY PEOPLE ★ ★

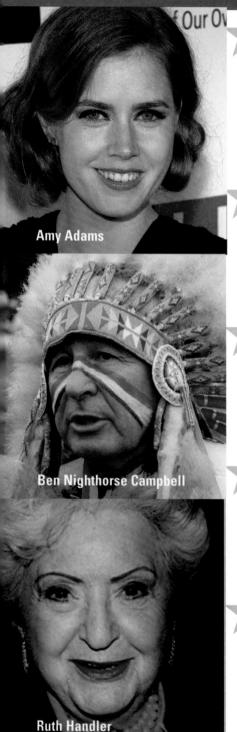

Amy Adams

Ben Nighthorse Campbell

Ruth Handler

1. Amy Adams

Amy Adams grew up in Colorado. In school, Adams participated in theater. She later moved to Los Angeles, where she landed roles in movies such as *Catch Me If You Can*, *Junebug*, and *Enchanted*. As of 2014, she has been nominated for four Academy Awards.

2. Tim Allen

Tim Allen, who was born in Denver in 1953, began his career as a standup comic. He went on to star in the hit television show *Home Improvement*. He is the voice of Buzz Lightyear in Disney's *Toy Story* films.

3. Ben Nighthorse Campbell

Colorado senator Ben Nighthorse Campbell was born in California in 1933 and moved to the Southern Ute Indian Reservation in 1977. In 1992, he became the first Native American in 60 years to be seated in the U.S. Senate.

4. M. Scott Carpenter

M. Scott Carpenter was born in Boulder in 1925. In 1962, he became the second astronaut to orbit Earth. Three years later, he went from space to the sea. He lived and worked on the ocean floor in the Navy's Sealab II project.

5. Ruth Handler

Ruth Handler, who was born in Denver in 1916, created a new kind of doll. Her doll was a teenager, complete with makeup and high heels. Handler's Barbie doll first appeared in 1959 at a toy industry trade show and went on to become one of the best-selling toys of all time.

COLORADO ★ ★ ★ ★

6. Ken Kesey

Born in La Junta in 1935, Ken Kesey was one of the voices of the 1960s hippie generation. After college, Kesey worked as an aide in a psychiatric hospital. This experience inspired his most famous novel, *One Flew Over the Cuckoo's Nest*.

7. Hattie McDaniel

Hattie McDaniel was born June 10, 1895, in Kansas, and moved to Denver in 1901. She was the first African-American woman to sing on the radio in the U.S., on Denver's KOA in 1925, and the first African-American to win an Oscar (best supporting actress) for her role as Mammy in *Gone With the Wind* in 1940.

8. Florence Sabin

Florence R. Sabin was born in Central City in 1871. She graduated from Johns Hopkins Medical School, and was the first woman to become a full professor there. Sabin studied the human body and did important medical research.

9. India Arie Simpson

India Arie is an award-winning musician and songwriter. Born in Denver, she released her first album in 2001. Since then, India Arie has won four Grammy awards, and has sold more than 10 million albums worldwide.

10. Amy Van Dyken

Amy Van Dyken, who was born in Englewood 1973, suffered from severe asthma as a child. When Van Dyken was six, her doctor suggested she take up swimming to improve her condition. In 1996, Van Dyken became the first American woman to win four gold medals at one Olympic Games.

Ken Kesey

India Arie Simpson

Amy Van Dyken

Who Coloradans Are

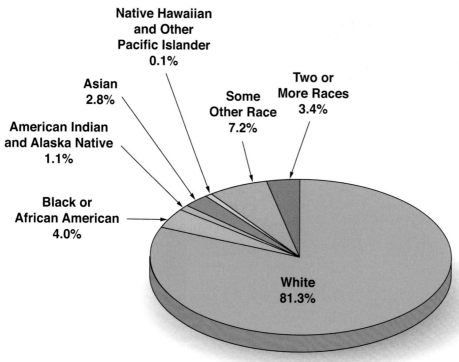

Native Hawaiian and Other Pacific Islander 0.1%

Asian 2.8%

American Indian and Alaska Native 1.1%

Black or African American 4.0%

Some Other Race 7.2%

Two or More Races 3.4%

White 81.3%

Total Population 5,029,196

Hispanic or Latino (of any race):

• 1,038,687 people (20.7%)

Note: The pie chart shows the racial breakdown of the state's population based on the categories used by the U.S. Bureau of the Census. The Census Bureau reports information for Hispanics or Latinos separately, since they may be of any race. Percentages in the pie chart may not add to 100 because of rounding.

Source: U.S. Bureau of the Census, 2010 Census

A Diverse Citizenry

According to the 2010 Census, Hispanics accounted for almost 21 percent of Colorado's population. Hispanics are people whose families come from places such as Mexico, Central America, the Caribbean, South America, or Spain. The majority of Colorado's Hispanics, more than 757,000, were of Mexican descent.

African Americans make up about 4 percent of the population, and almost 3 percent of Coloradans are of Asian descent. This includes Asian Indians, as well as people from China, Japan, Korea, Vietnam, and the Philippines.

Statewide percentages can be misleading, though. They show very little about how people actually live. Minorities are not scattered evenly across the state. Some areas have almost no minority population. Other areas have thriving communities of one or more minority groups.

In Colorado, a variety of programs and organizations are available to help newcomers from foreign nations. **Immigrants** can find everything from medical and mental health services to English classes, job training, and legal aid. Schools offer special programs for immigrant students and their families. For example, school districts are hiring bilingual and multilingual staff members to help parents with questions about their children's education. They are setting up multicultural education programs in schools with large numbers of immigrant children.

Children from an elementary school in Littleton reenact a Civl War battle in Chatfield State Park.

Education is an important issue for many Colorado residents.

Education: A Colorado Issue

Regardless of where they come from or how long they have been living in the state, many Colorado residents see education as an important issue. During local and state elections, citizens often take the politicians' views on education into account when voting. During votes for town or city budgets, many voters are often in favor of giving large amounts of money to the public school systems. Coloradans want to ensure that the public schools are able to offer young residents a high level of education, enough teachers, and enough resources.

Bilingual education has become a **controversial** topic in Colorado schools. The idea behind bilingual education seems simple, but there are many viewpoints. Bilingual education would allow students who do not speak English to study subjects such as history and science in their native language.

Supporters of bilingual education believe that this is the best option because students would not fall behind in their studies while they are learning English. Opponents believe that bilingual education slows down students' progress in English. They argue that some students would not learn English at all, but continue to rely on their native language. The additional expense of hiring bilingual educators is also a concern. Some people believe that the money should be used for resources that all students in the schools could use.

The bilingual education debate is over methods, not goals. Both sides agree that English fluency is important. Without it, students have a difficult time attending college and finding jobs. Opponents of bilingual education proposed new laws that would nearly eliminate it in Colorado schools. The most recent anti-bilingual laws were defeated. However, this issue will continue to affect the state.

A teacher helps students in Spanish class.

10 KEY EVENTS ★ ★ ★

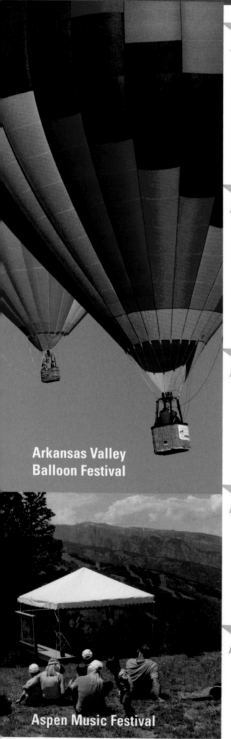

Arkansas Valley Balloon Festival

Aspen Music Festival

1. Arkansas Valley Balloon Festival

During the first weekend in November, the autumn sky is alive with soaring balloons, as ballooning enthusiasts and spectators gather for three days of festivities. With plenty of food and activities for the whole family, spectators have as much fun as the balloonists.

2. Aspen Music Festival

Every summer, classical music enthusiasts attend the nine-week Aspen Music Festival. They gather under an enormous tent that gives the concerts a "music under the stars" flavor. The 350 events include concerts, classes, lectures, and even kids' programs.

3. Cinco de Mayo Festival

Cinco de Mayo celebrates a Mexican victory over French invasion forces on May 5, 1862. Denver's Cinco de Mayo celebration draws half a million people who enjoy traditional Mexican music, food, and arts and crafts.

4. Colorado Dragon Boat Festival

Every summer, Chinese dragon boat races bring thousands of people to Sloan's Lake Park in Denver. The boats, with their bright dragon's heads and tails, hold up to twenty rowers, who time their strokes to the beating of a drum.

5. Colorado State Fair

Colorado's state fair is held in Pueblo every August. Residents and visitors watch and participate in a rodeo, races, parades, games, and concerts. The fair also hosts a fine arts show, livestock exhibitions, and cultural events.

★ COLORADO ★ ★ ★

6. Food & Wine Classic in Aspen

This event is held every June by *Food & Wine* magazine. It features cooking demonstrations, speakers, competitions, and of course, food and wine tastings by some of the world's most talented chefs.

7. Greeley Independence Stampede

The Greeley Independence Stampede bills itself as the World's Largest 4th of July Rodeo & Western Celebration. It features concerts, a carnival midway, flapjack feed, and a watermelon feast.

8. Leadville Boom Days

Every August, people gather in Leadville to celebrate the state's Old West history. Activities at this festival include mining contests, a motorcycle rodeo, burro races, music, and craft and food booths.

9. Pikes Peak Marathon

The Pikes Peak Marathon is the third oldest marathon in the United States. This 26.2-mile (42 km) race is considered one of the most difficult because of its dirt trails, rocks, and the 7,800-foot (2,377-m) ascent to the top of Pikes Peak.

10. Winter Carnival in Steamboat Springs

This annual winter event features ski racing, ski jumping, a shovel race, a dog sled pull, and even a high school marching band playing on skis! The highlight, though, is a large fireworks display.

Leadville Boom Days

Pikes Peak Marathon

Elected officials meet at Colorado's State Capitol in Denver.

How the Government Works

Colorado's constitution was adopted in 1876, when Colorado became a state. Though the constitution has been amended, or changed, over the years, it has never been replaced. Like the U.S. Constitution, Colorado's constitution describes the duties of the state government's three branches: the executive, the legislative, and the judicial. It remains the foundation for Colorado's entire system of government.

Levels of Government

Colorado's government begins at the local level, with towns, cities, and counties. The governing body of a town is called a board of trustees. The governing body of a city is called a council. Municipal (city and town) governments make **ordinances** (local laws), covering a variety of local concerns. For example, municipal governments can regulate traffic and parking on city streets. They can also separate business areas from residential areas with zoning ordinances. Cities and larger towns have municipal courts to deal with minor crimes and violations of local laws.

Cities and towns are part of counties. Colorado's 64 counties are responsible for carrying out state programs on a local level. Counties are governed by a board of elected commissioners. Other offices within the county include tax assessor, treasurer, and sheriff.

Senator Michael Bennet answers questions from residents at a Town Hall meeting in Denver.

Branches of Government

Executive

The executive branch consists of the governor, lieutenant governor, and different departments that cover various aspects of public life. The secretary of state, attorney general, and treasurer, as well as the governor and lieutenant governor, are elected by voters. Other department heads are appointed by the governor, with the approval of the state senate. Elected officials in the executive branch serve four-year terms. They cannot serve more than two consecutive terms.

Legislative

Colorado's legislature, or lawmaking body, is called the general assembly. It is made up of two houses. The senate has thirty-six members, and the house of representatives has sixty-five members. Members of the senate serve four-year terms and cannot hold office for more than two consecutive terms. Members of the house of representatives serve two-year terms and may be elected for up to four consecutive terms. Any proposed law must be passed by a majority vote in both houses of the legislature before it goes to the governor for executive approval.

Governor John Hickenlooper discusses Colorado education in Washington, D.C.

A view of the senate chamber inside Colorado's Capitol Building.

Judicial

The judicial branch enforces the laws of the state. Colorado's court system ranges from municipal (city) and county courts up to the state supreme court. State judges are not elected. They are appointed by the governor. However, during general elections, voters get to decide whether or not to retain the judges. District court judges appear on the ballot every six years. Appeals judges are up for approval every eight years, and supreme court judges are up every ten years.

Home Rule

In Colorado, local governments can elect to have home rule, which gives them more control over local matters. Home rule communities can tailor government policies to their particular needs. They can create their own budget guidelines and zoning regulations. Colorado has close to 100 cities and towns that are home rule municipalities. The largest is Colorado Springs.

Federal and statewide laws still apply, which places some practical limits on what home rule communities can do. For example, home rule communities must budget for state-mandated (that is, state-ordered) programs before they fund their own projects.

How a Bill Becomes a Law

Sometimes a state resident, official, or legislator comes up with an idea for a new state law. The idea is then passed on to a member of the general assembly. The reason is that only a state senator or state representative can officially introduce proposals for new laws. The proposed law is a written document called a bill. A bill can be introduced in either house. The bill is given a number and placed on the schedule of the house that will consider it first. On the appointed day, the bill's sponsor introduces it on the floor.

After this first reading, the bill is assigned to a committee for complete review. Which committee is assigned to analyze a bill depends upon the topic of that bill. For example, a senate bill about water conservation would go to the Committee on Agriculture and Natural Resources. A house bill on the same topic would go to the Committee on Agriculture, Livestock, and Natural Resources.

After studying the bill, the committee may postpone it, amend certain parts, or recommend it for passage. Unless a bill is postponed, it will go back to the floor (the entire legislative body) for a second reading. The entire senate or house discusses, debates, and proposes additional amendments to the bill. After this process, they vote. The bill may be accepted as amended, rejected, held over to another day, or sent back to the committee for additional work.

Bills that pass the committee process go on to a yet another reading. After this third reading, there is a final vote. If a bill passes the final vote, it is introduced to the second house, where the whole process is repeated.

Even when a bill is passed by both houses, the legislators' task may not be done. It often happens that the house and senate adopt different versions of the bill. In these cases, the differences must be fixed before a final version of the bill goes to the governor for his or her signature.

The governor can accept or reject the bill. If the governor signs the bill, it becomes law. If the governor vetoes—or rejects—the bill, it can still pass as long as three-fourths of both houses vote for the law.

Michael Hancock: Mayor of Denver, 2011-

Born in Texas in 1969, Hancock's family moved to Denver when he was just a baby. His interest in politics started early, and he started working right after high school. Hancock became the youngest president of an Urban League chapter, and then served as city council president. In 2011, he became Denver's second African American mayor.

John Kerry: U.S. Secretary of State, 2013-

Born in Denver in 1943, Kerry studied political science in college and then served during the Vietnam War. He was elected to the U.S. Senate in 1984, where he served until 2013. While serving, Kerry ran for president of the United States, but lost to George W. Bush. In 2012, Kerry was nominated as U.S. Secretary of State by President Barack Obama.

Dana Perino: White House Press Secretary, 2007-2009

Dana Perino was born in Wyoming in 1972, but she grew up in Denver. In college, Perino studied communications and political science. After school, she worked for several Washington, D.C. politicians. She became Deputy Press Secretary in 2005, and took over as Press Secretary in 2007.

COLORADO
YOU CAN MAKE A DIFFERENCE

★ Contacting Lawmakers

If you are interested in learning about Colorado's legislators, you can go to this website:

www.leg.state.co.us

There, you will find information about current legislation and contact information for state senators and representatives. On the left side, click "Contact Information." Directories are listed under both "House" and "Senate." You can also view maps of Colorado's different districts.

★ Making a Difference

Coloradans are known for taking an active interest in government and social issues. People of all ages become involved in many ways. To honor young people who make a difference in their communities, Colorado children's author T. A. Barron founded the Gloria Barron Prize for Young Heroes. Every year, ten outstanding achievers are recognized—five for their efforts on behalf of their communities and fellow beings, and five for their efforts on behalf of the environment. In 2001, the first year the awards were given out, they went to ten kids from Colorado. The next year, the judging was expanded to include kids from all over the country. Coloradans continue to make the cut. Past winners include a twelve-year-old Boulder girl who organized Showers to Go. This program gave free personal-care kits to homeless people. A thirteen-year-old girl from Evergreen founded an organization that provides education, food, and clothing to girls in a Peruvian orphanage. A thirteen-year-old Denver boy organized a bowl-a-thon that raised $9,000 to help a young burn victim's family with its medical bills. These students knew their projects would not solve the problem of health-care costs or homelessness. But they saw a need and found a way to help.

Workers prepare to move a manned spacecraft at Lockheed Martin, an aerospace company in Colorado.

Making a Living

For many years, agriculture and mining were the mainstays of Colorado's economy. That began to change in the mid–twentieth century as technology and service industries grew in importance. The service industry includes business, professional, medical, and consumer services. Manufacturing and transportation continue to be important, and tourism has grown along with the service and technology industries.

Colorado's New Economy

Agriculture, mining, and manufacturing are part of what is sometimes called the Old Economy. This economy was created by the farm, the mine, and the factory. The New Economy is created by computers, the Internet, and other new technologies.

These new technologies will not replace Colorado's Old Economy; they will coexist with it. In fact, technology benefits the Old Economy in many ways. Technology can make operations more efficient and less costly. For example, farmers in eastern Colorado can now computerize their business records, track crop prices and weather systems online, and carry cell phones out to the farthest reaches of their property. Farmers can also use advanced computer systems to map their fields and track the success of crops and irrigation techniques.

Agriculture

Some of Colorado's leading crops are potatoes, onions, peaches, and apples. Agriculture contributes more than $7 billion to the state economy each year.

Some enterprising farmers in Colorado have turned their cornfields into tourist attractions. One of these farmers, Bill English, created a large maze by planting 11 acres (4 ha) of corn in the shape of the Colorado state seal. Hundreds of visitors paid admission to try their luck at navigating the twists and turns of this designer cornfield. Other farmers have created corn mazes in different designs for family fun.

In western Colorado around Grand Junction, farmers grow wine grapes and other fruits such as apples, peaches, apricots, and cherries. These crops are sold throughout the state and to the rest of the country. Some of the produce is packaged or used in food-processing factories in the state.

In both eastern and western Colorado, raising livestock is more profitable than crop farming. In fact, 59 percent of Colorado's agricultural production came from livestock and livestock products in 2011. The raising of cattle and calves provided more than 40 percent of the state's agricultural revenue.

Another profitable area for farmers is specialty crops. Small farmers in particular have found that crops such as herbs, ornamental plants, and sod for lawns earn more than traditional field crops such as wheat and corn.

Mining

The days of "Pikes Peak or Bust" are long gone. But mining remains an important industry in Colorado. Coal is an important resource to Colorado, which ranks ninth among U.S. states in coal production. In 2012, twenty-nine million tons (twenty-six million metric tons) of coal were mined in the state, with a value of $1.1 billion.

Colorado mines produce millions of tons of other minerals, including gypsum, limestone, molybdenum, titanium, and uranium. Molybdenum is used as an alloy in stainless steel. It makes the steel tougher, harder, and more able to resist corrosion. Colorado is the leading producer of this metal in the United States. Gunnison County, Colorado, is also home to the largest reserves of titanium in the United States.

Although Colorado is no longer experiencing a gold rush, the state still ranks fourth in the country (behind Nevada, Alaska, and Utah) in gold production. In 2011, Colorado produced an estimated 267,172 troy ounces (8,310 kg) of this precious metal.

Manufacturing

Manufacturing is the process of taking raw materials (such as cotton) and adding value to them by turning them into finished products (such as cloth). Products manufactured in Colorado include scientific instruments, such as medical devices and electronic equipment, as well as machinery, such as computers and communications equipment. The state also has a large food processing industry. This includes meatpacking, production of animal feed, and brewing. The Coors Brewing Company in Golden, Colorado, has been in operation since 1873. The company employs thousands of people and produces billions of barrels of beer every year.

Colorado is also leading the county in "green" manufacturing. In March 2008, Danish energy company Vestas opened—in Windsor, Colorado—the first U.S. factory to manufacture blades for wind turbines. These modern-day windmills are used to generate electricity. Wind energy—a "clean" energy source—is one of the fastest-growing energy sources in the world today.

In 2009, Vestas broke ground on two new factories in Brighton, another blade facility and a nacelle assembly plant. (The nacelle is mounted on the top of the turbine and houses parts including the gearbox, generator, controller, and brake.) The plants employ thousands of people among them. Vestas also built a plant in Pueblo to manufacture the towers for wind turbines. The factory is one of the largest of its kind in the world.

This Colorado cornfield has been made into a maze. Corn is one of the state's most important crops.

★ 10 ★ KEY INDUSTRIES ★

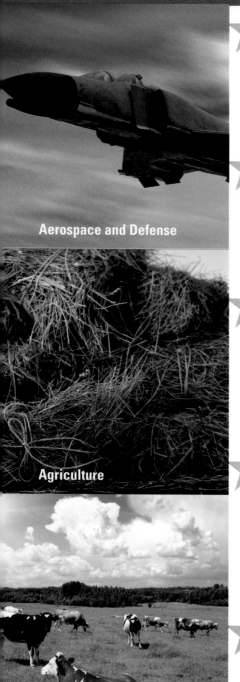

Aerospace and Defense

Agriculture

Cattle

1. Aerospace and Defense

Colorado's aerospace industry ranks second in the nation for private aerospace employment. Many of the country's major aerospace companies, including Ball Aerospace, Boeing, Lockheed Martin, and Northrop Grumman, have locations there.

2. Agriculture

Agriculture and food generate more than $5 billion annually. The largest crops in Colorado include corn, wheat, hay, and potatoes. The hay, and some of the corn, is used to feed livestock in the state and is also sent to other parts of the country.

3. Cattle

Colorado cattle and calves account for more than 60 percent of the state's agricultural products. The beef is sold within the state, across the country, and around the world. Colorado ranchers export beef to places such as Japan, the United Kingdom, and Canada.

4. Coal

Colorado coal is taken from the western stretches of the state. It is burned for heating and generating electricity. It supplies about 72 percent of Colorado's electricity. The total value of coal produced in Colorado in 2012 is estimated to be $1.1 billion.

5. Defense

Colorado is home to several military installations, such as Buckley Air Force Base, the United States Air Force Academy, North American Defense Command (NORAD), and U.S. Northern Command (USNORTHCOM). The military in Colorado employs more than 70,000 people.

COLORADO

6. Electronics

More than 300 companies exist in Colorado that provide electronics products, parts, and services. In 2012, Arrow Electronics, an electronics distribution and services company, was named one of "the world's most admired companies" for the 12th year in a row by *Forbes* magazine.

7. Energy

Colorado is a leader in energy conservation, clean energy, and new energy techniques. The state promotes development of energy using solar power, wind, natural gas, oil, coal, and biofuels. Colorado has a goal of using 30 percent renewable energy by 2020.

8. Greenhouses/Nurseries

Besides growing crops to feed people and animals, Colorado farms are used to grow plants and flowers. Greenhouses and nurseries across the state grow small trees, flowers, and shrubs that are sent to florists in the state and around the country. Many greenhouses are also used for plant research.

9. Office Equipment

Some Colorado factories make office products, such as computers and other electronics. Research companies based in the state use new technologies to develop new machines and products.

10. Tourism/Skiing

Colorado's resorts are perfect for skiing, snowboarding, or snowmobiling. The ski industry alone accounts for nearly $2 billion of Colorado's income. Every year more than eleven million people come to Colorado to ski and snowboard.

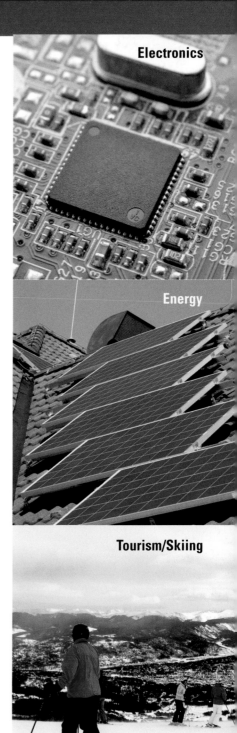

Electronics

Energy

Tourism/Skiing

Recipe for Mini Cheeseburgers

Coloradoans love eating meat. From beef, chicken, and turkey to buffalo, elk, and caribou, you are sure to find something meaty and interesting on a menu there. You do not have to go to Colorado, though, to eat something tasty. With the help of an adult, you can make these mini cheeseburgers at home!

What You Need

1 pound (450 g) ground beef

1/4 teaspoon (1 ml) salt

1/4 teaspoon (1 ml) pepper

Mini burger buns

Tomatoes

Lettuce

Cheese

Grill pan

What to Do

- An adult should oil the grill pan, and heat it over medium-high heat until hot.
- Flavor the ground beef by adding salt and pepper. Mix it together with your hands. (Remember to always clean your hands before and after handling raw meat.)

- Roll the ground meat into 8 equal-size balls. Gently press them down to make patties. Place them on a plate. Wash your hands.
- Rinse the tomatoes and lettuce in cold water. Have an adult help you cut the tomatoes into slices.
- An adult should cook the burgers for 6 minutes, and then turn them over. If you want cheese, put cheese slices on top. Grill the burgers about 6 minutes more, until they are cooked through.
- Remove burgers from the grill pan and place them on a clean plate. Let the burgers sit for 2 to 3 minutes.
- Arrange the burgers on the buns, and add your favorite toppings!

Wholesale and Retail Trade

Wholesalers are the link between manufacturers who make the merchandise and retailers who sell to the general public. Wholesalers buy from manufacturers in large quantities and then sell smaller quantities to retailers, who in turn sell the products to consumers. About 2.7 percent of Colorado's workforce is employed in wholesale trade, while 11.3 percent work in retail.

The retail industry includes everything from restaurants and bars to supermarkets, department stores, and specialty shops. In addition to day-to-day retail establishments, such as gas stations, supermarkets, and pharmacies, Denver and other cities have major centers that transform shopping into a recreational activity.

For example, Denver's Cherry Creek neighborhood has tree-lined streets with more than 320 businesses, including department stores, specialty shops, art galleries, and restaurants. Locals and tourists alike enjoy spending time at Cherry Creek, browsing in shops or eating in the restaurants. Businesses like these help the economy in a few ways. The stores provide a place to sell products manufactured in Colorado. The jobs created by these stores and restaurants keep many Coloradans employed. The taxes that consumers pay when purchasing from these businesses go back to the state.

Service Industries

A service is an activity or process that one person performs for another. It does not transfer ownership of any physical object. A business that rents cars is a service, while one that sells them is not.

Service industries include everything from banking and insurance to health care, education, transportation, and communications. In addition to these, thousands of providers offer personal and domestic services such as hair styling, child care, and home improvement.

Technology has created many new service jobs. For example, many Coloradans are making a living by programming computers, designing web pages, installing digital television cable, or performing other technical services.

In 1999, Colorado's general assembly created a new agency: the Governor's Office of Innovation and Technology (OIT). The mission of this office is to attract high-technology

A research technician prepares a wind turbine gearbox for testing. Wind energy is a "clean" energy source.

industries to the state, develop training programs to expand the technology workforce, and create a high-speed **fiber optic** network to streamline government operations.

Tourism and Recreational Services

Colorado has a thriving tourist industry. There are more than 144,000 people working in the tourism industry, which makes it the largest employer in the state. Altogether, tourism adds almost $15 billion a year to the Colorado economy.

In winter, people come from all over the world to the state's ski resorts. In summer, they come for camping, river rafting, rock climbing, and many other outdoor activities.

Every year more than 4 million people visit Colorado's four national parks: Rocky Mountain, Mesa Verde, Great Sand Dunes, and Black Canyon of the Gunnison. There, they can experience some of the most incredible natural and cultural wonders the country has to offer, including the highest sand dunes in North America, one of the deepest canyons in the Western Hemisphere, and, of course, the magnificent cliff dwellings of the Ancestral Pueblo people. The state also has 41 state parks, which provide amazing opportunities for outdoor recreation and adventure.

Many people also visit Colorado for its professional sports teams. The Denver Nuggets are the state's NBA team. Invesco Field at Mile High is home to the Denver Broncos football team. hockey fans attend the games played by the state's NHL team, the Colorado Avalanche. The Colorado Rockies are the state's Major League Baseball team. Denver is the smallest metropolitan area in the United States to have professional teams in all four sports. The state's economy benefits from the money spent on game tickets and souvenirs.

Taking Care of Colorado

Environmental protection has long been an important issue for Coloradans. There are laws and programs to preserve open spaces, protect endangered wildlife, and develop clean sources of energy. A group called the Colorado Renewable Energy Society (CRES) develops plans to help conserve energy and use renewable resources such as wind and solar power.

Colorado already leads the nation in wind-energy production. As of 2013, the state had more than 1,500 wind turbines that provided 2,300 megawatts of electricity. That is enough to power about 800,000 homes. Around 11 percent of Colorado's electricity is provided by wind.

One of the state's most difficult resource management problems is also one of the oldest: water. In this semiarid state, there never seems to be enough of it, and the distribution is uneven. Most of the state's water comes from the mountains. The state's annual precipitation is generally less than 20 inches (50 cm), with the driest areas receiving only 10 inches (25 cm). In the mountains, the highest elevations may receive as much as 50 inches (125 cm) per year.

Colorado has an advanced system of dams, tunnels, and reservoirs to distribute and conserve water resources. Even with all the planning and technology, droughts are a constant danger. In very dry years, Coloradans may face mandatory water rationing.

Looking Forward

Coloradans are aware that the unique beauty of their state is an economic asset. It is the foundation for their high quality of life, and the reason that millions of people visit the state each year. Preserving the beauty of the landscape while continuing to develop a variety of industries will be Colorado's challenge for the twenty-first century.

COLORADO
STATE MAP

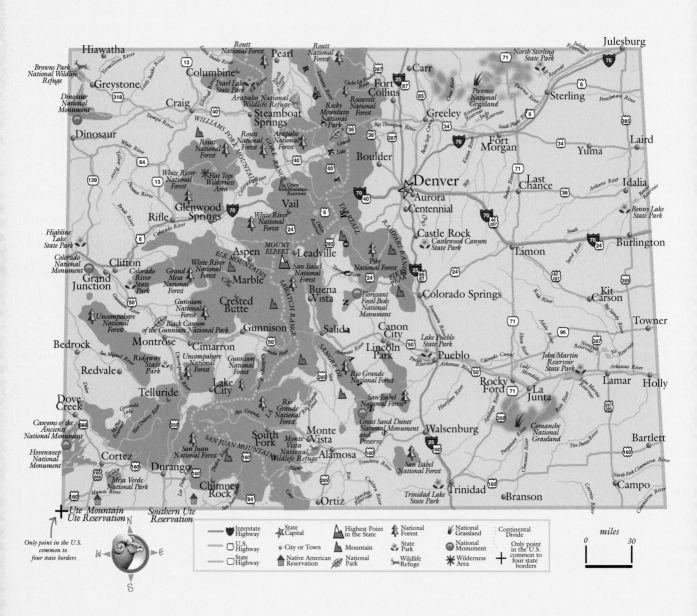

Hiawatha

Browns Park
National Wildlife
Refuge

Greystone

318

Dinosaur
National
Monument

Dinosaur

64

139

Craig

40

Columbine

13

Pearl

Routt
National Forest

Pearl Lake
State Park

Arapaho National
Wildlife Refuge

Steamboat
Springs

Routt
National
Forest

Routt
National
Forest

Rocky
Mountain
National
Park

Roosevelt
National
Forest

Fort
Collins

287

25

87

85

34

Carr

Greeley

Pawnee
National
Grassland

North Sterling
State Park

71

76

Sterling

6

Julesburg

Julesburg

385

Laird

White River
National
Forest

Flat Tops
Wilderness
Area

Green
Mountain
Reservoir

36

35

287

Boulder

40

Denver

70

40

Aurora
Centennial

34

76

Fort
Morgan

Last
Chance

71

Yuma

34

Idalia

36

Bonny Lake
State Park

Rifle

Glenwood
Springs

70

6

White River
National
Forest

Vail

6

24

Castle Rock

Castlewood Canyon
State Park

70

40

287

Limon

70

24

Burlington

Highline
Lake
State Park

Colorado
National
Monument

Clifton

Grand
Junction

50

Colorado
River
State
Park

Marble

Aspen

Grand
Mesa
National
Forest

White River
National
Forest

ELK MOUNTAINS

MOUNT
ELBERT

Leadville

285

San Isabel
National
Forest

24

Pike
National Forest

PIKES PEAK

25

85

87

24

Colorado Springs

Florissant
Fossil Beds
National
Monument

Kit
Carson

385

Towner

Crested
Butte

Gunnison
National
Forest

Montrose

Cimarron

Ridgway
State
Park

Uncompahgre
National
Forest

Gunnison
National
Forest

Buena
Vista

Gunnison

50

Salida

Lincoln
Park

Canon
City

50

Lake Pueblo
State Park

96

Pueblo

John Martin
Reservoir
State Park

Lamar

Holly

Bedrock

Redvale

Black Canyon
of the Gunnison National Park

Uncompahgre
National
Forest

Lake
City

Rio Grande
National
Forest

San Isabel
National Forest

Rocky
Ford

La
Junta

71

350

Comanche
National
Grassland

Bartlett

160

Dove
Creek

Canyons of the
Ancients
National Monument

666

Telluride

550

Rio
Grande
National
Forest

San Juan
National Forest

South
Fork

Monte
Vista
National
Wildlife Refuge

Monte
Vista

160

Alamosa

160

Great Sand Dunes
National Monument
and
Preserve

San Isabel
National Forest

Walsenburg

25

160

Trinidad Lake
State Park

Trinidad

160

Branson

Campo

160

Hovenweep
National
Monument

Cortez

Durango

160

Mesa Verde
National Park

160
666

Chimney
Rock

84

Ortiz

285

Ute Mountain
Ute Reservation

Southern Ute
Reservation

Only point in the U.S.
common to
four state borders

N

W   E

S

Interstate
Highway

U.S.
Highway

State
Highway

State
Capital

City or Town

Native American
Reservation

Highest Point
in the State

Mountain

National
Park

National
Forest

State
Park

Wildlife
Refuge

National
Grassland

National
Monument

Wilderness
Area

Continental
Divide

Only point in the U.S.
common to
four state
borders

miles

0   30

COLORADO
MAP SKILLS

1. What is Colorado's highest point?

2. What Native American reservation is located south of Cortez?

3. What interstate highway runs north-south through the middle of the state?

4. Which National Monument can you find near Greystone?

5. What U.S. highway runs between Montrose and Durango?

6. Which mountain range is located south of Aspen?

7. What is the name of the national grassland that is located in northeast Colorado?

8. Hiawatha is near what river?

9. What highway would you take when traveling from Denver to Glenwood Springs?

10. Steamboat Springs is located near what wildlife refuge?

Great Sand Dunes National Monument

South Platte River

Vail

1. Mount Elbert
2. Ute Reservation
3. Interstate 25
4. Dinosaur National Monument
5. U.S. Highway 550
6. Elk Mountains
7. Pawnee National Grassland
8. Vermillion River
9. U.S. Highway 70
10. Arapaho National Wildlife Refuge

State Seal, Flag, and Song

Colorado's state seal features a shield with three snow-capped mountains and mining tools. Below the shield is the state motto in Latin, which translates to "Nothing Without the Deity." A pyramid with the eye of God and a bundle of wooden rods with an ax are located above the shield. The bundle of rods represents the strength lacking in a single rod; the ax symbolizes authority and leadership. Colorado's year of statehood, 1876, is displayed at the bottom of the seal.

Colorado's state flag was adopted in 1911. It has two blue stripes and one white stripe. The flag features a large red C surrounding a golden disk. The blue represents the sky, the gold stands for sunshine, the white represents the snow-topped mountains, and the red represents the color of Colorado rock. The yellow and white of the flag also represent Colorado's history of gold and silver deposits, which brought many settlers to the area.

On May 8, 1915, Colorado named "Where the Columbines Grow," by A.J. Flynn, the state song. Find the lyrics at **www.netstate.com/states/symb/song/co_song.htm**. The state added John Denver's "Rocky Mountain High" as a second state song in March 2007. Find the lyrics at **www.statesymbolsusa.org/Colorado/stateSONGdenver.html**.

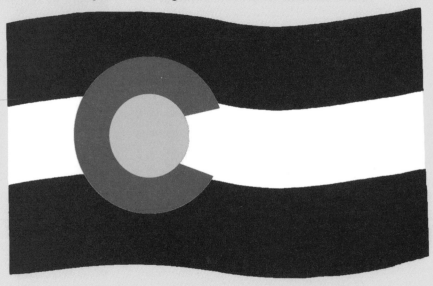

Glossary

altitude　　The vertical elevation of an object above a surface (as sea level or land).

ancestors　　People who were in someone's family in past times.

conservation　　The protection of animals, plants, and natural resources.

controversial　　Likely to produce discussion, disagreement, or argument.

deciduous　　Having leaves that fall off every year.

descendants　　People who are related to a person or group of people who lived in the past.

encroach　　To advance beyond the usual or proper limits.

erosion　　The gradual destruction of something by natural forces (such as water, wind, or ice).

fiber optic　　The branch of optics that deals with the transmission of light through transparent fibers, as in the form of pulses for the transmission of data or communications, or through fiber bundles for the transmission of images.

immigrants　　People who come to a country to live there.

irrigation　　The watering of land by artificial means to promote plant growth.

legislature　　A group of people with the power to make or change laws.

mesas　　Hills that have flat tops and steep sides.

ordinances　　Laws or regulations made by a city or town government.

plateau　　A large flat area of land that is higher than other areas of land that surround it.

prospectors　　People searching for gold or silver.

scholars　　People who have studied particular subjects for a long period of time and know a lot about them.

More About Colorado

BOOKS

Aloian, Molly. *The Rocky Mountains*. New York, NY: Crabtree Publishing, 2011.

Cunningham, Kevin. *The Ute*. New York, NY: Scholastic, 2011.

Schnobrich, Emily. *Colorado: The Centennial State*. Minneapolis, MN: Bellwether Media, 2013.

Somervill, Barbara A. *Colorado (America the Beautiful)*. New York, NY: Scholastic, 2014.

WEBSITES

Colorado State Parks:

www.parks.state.co.us

The Official Colorado State Website:

www.colorado.gov

The Official Site for Colorado Travel and Tourism:

www.colorado.com

ABOUT THE AUTHORS

Linda Jacobs Altman has written many books for young people. She and her husband live in a small California town near a lake, with a house full of dogs, cats, and birds.

Stephanie Fitzgerald has been writing nonfiction for children for more than ten years, and she is the author of more than twenty books. Her specialties include history, wildlife, and popular culture. Stephanie lives in Stamford, Connecticut, with her husband and their daughter.

Index

Page numbers in **boldface** are illustrations.

Index